Lee Upton

Undid in the Land of Undone

New Issues Poetry & Prose

A Green Rose Book

New Issues Poetry & Prose
The College of Arts and Sciences
Western Michigan University
Kalamazoo, Michigan 49008

An Inland Seas Poetry Book

 Inland Seas poetry books are supported by a grant from

The Michigan Council for Arts and Cultural Affairs.

First Edition, 2007.

ISBN-10   1-930974-72-8 (paperbound)
ISBN-13   978-1-930974-72-2 (paperbound)

Library of Congress Cataloging-in-Publication Data:
Upton, Lee
Undid in the Land of Undone/Lee Upton
Library of Congress Control Number: 2007924971

Managing Editor   Marianne Swierenga
Copy Editor   Elizabeth Marzoni
Designer   Laura Hervey
Art Director   Tricia Hennessy
Production Manager   Paul Sizer
                         The Design Center, School of Art
                         College of Fine Arts
                         Western Michigan University

Undid in the Land of Undone

Lee Upton

New Issues

WESTERN MICHIGAN UNIVERSITY

Also by Lee Upton

Poetry:

The Invention of Kindness
No Mercy
Approximate Darling
Civilian Histories

Literary Criticism:

Jean Garrigue: A Poetics of Plenitude
Obsession and Release: Rereading the Poetry of Louise Bogan
The Muse of Abandonment: Origin, Identity, Mastery in Five American Poets
Defensive Measures: The Poetry of Niedecker, Bishop, Glück, and Carson

for Eric Ziolkowski
—again and always

Contents

VI.

I.

Dyserotica

There is utopia
and there is dystopia.
There is erotica

and there is . . .
what you've written.
Somehow—

as if what two
at a minimum
people might do

or could do
in another lifetime—
if suddenly shipwrecked, for instance,

or if it was the end of the world
and they alone were left to procreate—
as if your words must be

the antidote to desire,
the corrective trip to the morgue,
the inoculation we haven't been waiting for . . .

although even your dyserotica
becomes erotic for some of us:
what else are death bed

confessions for?
Forgive me for not being impressed
by your image of spiders

crawling the mouth of Aphrodite.
I know you don't love me,
but why do you have to brag about it?

The Table

To rise from the table
he put his hands upon it—
ate and drank
and played cards upon it.
Wrote to his mother,
blessed her,
made politics upon it,
pressed the fly leaf,
let poinsettias yellow upon it,
dropped the bread and killed the crust upon it,
read his Edgar Allan Poe upon it,
sponged the boards and tumblers,
wedged and split
the knife upon it

but when he turned the table over,
its four legs up in the air
like a dead horse,
that's when he ended our bargaining,
that's when he gripped more than the table
and took more than signals from across the table,
more than tappings, rustlings, eye blinks,
negotiation's soft wiring,
that's when he lunged over the legs of the table,
that's when at last—how long do I have to wait—
he turned over the precinct
and drafted his declaration and colonial address,
that's when nothing could go on under the table
and that's when he got the table to work.

Omniscient Love

He was in knocking range of my secrets.
He had found kelp there.
He nested in the coral beds.
In a past life he was born
to me as a set of twins.
He was applied to me as a topical ointment.
He was a prescient code,
a secret writing shaped into flesh.
He was the fathomer I never expected,
the pillow talk of the bureaucracy,
the breeze that could carry the world off-course.
It was as if we'd always believed in each other precisely,
and even the clouds agreed,
and the dog and his bone;
every particle of language
jumped like a flea around him. He was
a pirate's nautical exercise
and an argument for the resurrection.
He was in every seed bed
and digression.
He was bending down my angels and breasting
the seas of goldenmost wheat.
To ask for everything and get it
seemed a paltry thing
next to being recognized by him.
A button couldn't pop
but he was there with a net.

Ancient Art

Come Down, Dido

Off the pyre.
Forget the man.
Remember your résumé.

You should know enough
to step back
from anyone who says Relax.

Three months and you
won't want to sing a song about
him. Two years

and you'll ask "Who?"
Not that we ask you
to be sensible. His sail

turns to thread on the sea.
What's his hurry?
Come down, Dido.

What a past you've had.
Think about Carthage
and all that.

Cuckold in Three Parts

Pity the husband.
But so too the wife-stealer,
the Paris among us,

and Helen too—comical although
cast in a bitter comedy, less bitter
while some of the parties

are suitably young enough. Inevitably,
our sympathies turn,
and even the most curious know

to look away from grief's
messenger. Pleasure
is a messenger, not a god.

About the Greeks Bearing Gifts

We had ourselves to thank first—
our capacity for celebration, for
forgetfulness, for metaphor.

Things were not what they were.
Even the eye of the blind dog
turned into an oiled pearl and an island.

Whereas the Greeks hardly got
rid of their scent. Go ahead, blame us.
Our relief was foolhardy and certain.

But then, we were fertile in fools.
We hardly recognized ourselves
in the light of their gift.

To us it seems stupid
only in retrospect.
As if any people would abandon their art.

Another Return from Ithaca

Calypso dandled stupid young men by a fire.
Circe led swine in a drove.
Just as all her failures were,

Odysseus proved invisible to her.
The Cyclops had turned to bones
the size of a dinosaur's.

By then, the hero's only son
was sunk like a stick-in-the-mud,
afraid of his mother unraveling her tricks.

Neptune was no less a psychopath
than he ever was
and never stopped punking a navy in another war.

Adding a Detail to *The Garden of Delights*

In any couple one of the couple
must be in love with something not quite

remotely human,
or at best remotely human,

the strawberry prickling with hair,
the blueberry opening like a corpse

to a cascade of its own miniatures.
A cherry balanced perfectly on our heads.

Obviously it's time for
the garden to ferment.

Time to give to this sinister wine
the drift of scent

thriving in shade and dampness.
Bleached pelvis of the skeleton,

eye holes in a white mask,
perfection of suspended toxins:

Add, that is, the lily-of-the-valley,
baffled at breath,

the bent claw in the bone cup:
a defense of poetry.

The Cloud Eater

The bunting of the side stage curls up just as
Cassandra's throne is torn apart like the frays in egg drop soup.
But no, more violent—slit by arrows,
until a dune descends
and an estuary fills
to separate the brine from clouds filling with clouds,
to tighten far below the pleats of the mushroom,
until high above us a bridge, improvised,
pours into a dissolving mountain
and concusses through spume
as generations fill the gap where
a cloud meadow drifts,
waiting all this time until
ink is drawn up out of paper
to where a new cloud gathers itself and puckers like an
inoculation site,
and this—where did it leave us,
the lowest waterfall spilling arrows
below the summit,
below the charcoal drawing of reluctance—
or here on the slope of the facing mountain,
its newsprint sliding,
a portion of sky the color
of an ice chest harboring fish scales
and silt—all this
in a cupola where seasons speculate,
where the grey rust that is not so much a substance as a mark of abuse
without the persistence of a scar
turns into an airy flume,
a draft unending,
the storm slitting daylight, and we are not changed after all
as we look into the orchestra that surges
into sputtering liquid fire working its way
down toward us even as
the shovel crushes the white flame,
the brush spreads the ashes,
the electric eel twitches in icy beads—
making horizons in horizons,
as if seconds were made to be seen,
cream clotting in lemon, and
over the shaded edge
populations swell in synchronous air,

and then the whole prospect turns over, and we ask:
how did that spume start, that backward running funnel,
that timepiece over the peaks,
those evaporating age spots?—
and on this side why are we rowed past
an infinity of mist,
something past free—while
this, held aloft,
endures change,
emblems sliding into deeper emblems as
our endless greed for time is exposed,
and the belief, felt, intentioned,
that we have always been and never exactly started, at most unfolded into
this pouring avalanche of vapor
that tries the mind on
with the muslin of a tall dream,
beyond the roof of the mouth
or the high snow,
grey-eyed, green-tinged, dolphin-backed pantomime,
not the future but the past turned over,
advancing, loading up its ark and taking all our shapes.

II.

Sure

I'd call this place Hell
if it didn't sound so final.
I prefer: The Underworld:
Awe clapping its great wings above our heads.
My daughter read the hero's name without ever
having heard it said:
Useless, she informed us, blinded the Cyclops.
Useless: that's a name he might have liked,
next to Nobody, next to Walk-through-the-fires-of-the-dead.
First things first, he learned, usefully.
Back to the living,
the false world, the changing one
where customs differ,
where everyone wants certainty to last.
So, much later, a poet wrote of an infant god
whirling in flames:
Poor Robert Southwell.
First strung up, beheaded, gutted.

Plague Time

The fleas, squired
by rats, sophisticated by travel,
took Donne's lovers

with blood under their fingernails,
twitched up the legs
of gentlemen,

poached in hamlets,
snuggled into the family pelts,
the baby at the breast,

the old woman bedded in straw—
until at last snow churned against the lanterns
and nightmares swarmed

in bedclothes made of ice
and ghosts stood up
exhausted with rage—

until the breeze tingled
through the narrow slots
that passed for windows,

the snow melted,
the daffodils bent their heads—
and it is spring.

Unmistaken

Before he stole the girl he stole an old woman. A widow with
no one to attempt to save her, and no one,
at the last minute, to turn to see her sucked back into Hell.
It was another of his mistakes, everyone said. He disagreed.
He needed a mother for the girl? Or a grandmother?
No. He needed a living heart seeded with pain and grief. To taste.
Or he couldn't so much as stand up in Hell with any desire.
He couldn't have kept on getting to know his people.

Saturn and His Children

The flame was blown out on the lamp,
and you knocked over your wine glass,

and then the waitress re-lit the lamp.
Minutes later the flame blew out again.

Shark tail, shreddings of sea lettuce.
And what was most incredible to us yet:

a wined honey. What did we do
to deserve this? you asked.

Your face was half in some kind of netting,
and then a new flame shone in a pastry shell,

and the gravy went by in a salver,
and we stalled at the pudding,

soft at the center as a fontanel.
And then you were laughing and asked,

We've died, dear, do you think
we might as well enjoy it?

And next it was our father's turn,
and there weren't enough dishes.

It's good of you to ask permission,
we said before he began.

The Hedge

I trusted her for a dose of iniquity,
said from behind the hedge.
I sang like an artificial
bird of prey,

sung from behind the hedge.
I made so many mistakes, he said,
at least I wasn't about to swill
in piety—

whispered from behind the hedge.
His very skin,
vaguely amphibian—
behind the hedge.

The license to simulate
an occupation
behind the hedge.
All of us responsible

as pirates
behind the hedge,
sleek with ignorant
pleasures

behind the hedge.
You without a reputation worth
protecting
behind the hedge.

A unicorn goring a maiden
behind the hedge.
And the hedge?
The hedge itself so hedged

and pummeled—
it's worse than a fen.
A sponge in a bucket
after a night of revenge.

Satyr Without Desire

Unable to freeze hair with his curly breath,
to make clouds snap at a window,
to blanch the back of a neck.
The mud caked in his hooves

left no track. His head like a cauliflower,
his unquivering nostrils,
his goat eyelids.
No one wanted him.

As if every age since the Age of Reason
were the Age of Reason.
And yet I followed him into thickets
where he ignored me.

Unicorn's Horn

Coral upstart of the philosopher's letter,
the arrow indigenous to the forehead,
the never known, never seen, never touched,
outliving species after species wiped from the earth.
The unicorn sleeps in the virgin's lap
and rears up—
a fleck of blood in every raindrop—
himself indelible, not like his host—not like a dream,
not like a dream in which we commit a crime
and wake up guilty, and wounded with it.

The Autobiography of Irony

They cut a channel for the giant horse to drag their graves in upright.
A bee drowses in the ear of Plato's disciple in a cave.
The young virtuoso chooses suicide
and lives to kill her talent.

Commonly Said

If It Were Any Closer It Would Bite You

It's been wanting to bite you
throughout these many years.
If it happened to be any farther away
you might at last see it—
but then you would be tempted
to pretend you don't,
the way you are with people who cut you.

You should rise to the occasion,
if the occasion weren't so desperate to kick you.
But as for that thing—what you've been looking for?
If it were any closer it would bite you.
Of course it could wring your neck,
but it prefers to bite you.
The more it prefers you
the more teeth it has.

Who Died and Made You Queen?

We must have been four, five,
the first time we heard it.
But then we heard it for years.
We hadn't even known
there were airs to put on.
The worst thing:
to be seen to have ambition.
Even the quiet, the gentle,
the measly, the dim—
should ever in our lives we
climb to our thrones
and hold up our chins
someone said:
Who died and made you queen?
And we didn't say the obvious:
Who lived to make you their servant?

III.

Immortal Even More

In Ovid's Metamorphoses, Erysichthon orders his workmen to fell
an oak inhabited by a nymph and sacred to Ceres. Ceres punishes
him by rendering him insatiably hungry. In desperation, Erysichthon
attempts to sell his own daughter to feed himself. Neptune takes pity
on Erysichthon's daughter and allows her at will to be transformed
—to escape anyone who would possess her.

The leaves are more silver-veined than any others,
a poor people's god rustling

with millions of rumors,
shields flashing, pixels glaring.

Any man should look with awe
at the concussions above him,

that bomb blast of leaves, that irradiant.
Yet when every branch turns white

from blood loss
there is no stopping him.

Not even when ropes of blood
twist through the air,

spooling like honey from
the lip of a jar.

*

A story tells itself three times—
first to the teller,
another time to the listener,

another time to a god no one believes in.

The father can't be satisfied.
The daughter can't satisfy anyone.

No story yet has ever satisfied everyone.

She stood in the doorway,
his daughter who would become
any thing she pleased.

Don't come closer if
you know what's good for you,

both of them said.

*

He sees ladders and tables
and doors where others see God.

Blood spatters his face.
The dying girl's breath

volts into his lungs.
He killed one of god's voices.

What did he expect?
A satisfying meal after that?

*

And don't say *pimp*.

He needed her to take care of him.
The truth doesn't

care about origins,
doesn't care about its father.

His daughter became what she thought.
She should think of him,

then she'd know what hunger is.

When at last a horrible woman showed up
she turned out to be
someone from marketing, full of suggestions

for my father,
watching him at the table
where he was helpless.

I think she loved watching him:
he had a pursuit, a discipline.
The company we keep.

No, I wouldn't even
claim her as company.
She didn't know enough

to be ashamed.
She was shameless amazement,
an emptiness that looks.

But as for me, I wasn't myself.
I knew as much when the first buyer
talked to me as if I were a man.

I said truthfully:
I hadn't seen any girl at all.
I looked down at the salt burns on my palms.

It was because of my father's greed,
his insatiable need,
that this instant of joy was given to me.

*

Once there was a time
when my face betrayed me,
telling a story

as if there was
a collaborator in my house.
My body was a place

that kept naming me.
Then, I wanted invisibility.
Now I have something

better: visibility without consequences.
When I looked into my father's mouth
I saw an ordinary man's ordinary tongue.

Not the god who ruined him,
not a god spun and mirrored
at the back of his throat.

Not his suspicion,
his cynicism,
his hatred of the young.

Later, my father hardly spoke except to ask
what I'd brought him.
I hadn't tricked enough men on any one day.

He was always lifting a spoon.
It became a philosophy to him,
the philosophy of the spoon,

until he swallowed.
He didn't believe in what he couldn't see.
He didn't believe in what he could see.

My metamorphoses—
he believed in them
as some well prepared trick.

*

You think it's wrong to want so much?

I didn't want everything.

I wanted, first, not to have to change my mind.

Next, I wanted my daughter to help me.

Then, I wanted not to have to change my mind again.

I hear myself sing in the morning. The same song.

These words.

Now that I'm everywhere.

*

SO YOU'RE EVERYWHERE?
HERE I AM, A GOD, AND YOU'RE

TAKING UP MY IMMORTAL TIME.
AN ETERNAL LIFE FOR A GOD

IS NOT A CHOICE.

YOU'RE HUNGRY.
NOTHING CURES YOU.

THAT'S A SIMPLE DIAGNOSIS.
YOU KNOW YOUR WAY

AROUND YOURSELF.

YOU KNOW WHAT'S AT
THE CENTER OF THE TEMPLE.

WHAT GOD WOULD BORE HERSELF WITH ACCOUNTABILITY?
THE GOD OF DEATH?

DEATH DOESN'T NEED A GOD.

WAS HIS DAUGTHER COMPARABLE TO EVEN ONE OF US?
I'LL TELL YOU THE ANSWER:

A GOD DOESN'T NEED TO CHANGE FORM.
EVEN ZEUS. THERE ARE EASIER WAYS

TO HIDE ADULTERY.

LOOK AT THE HUMANS. GENERALLY
THEY'RE SUCCESSFUL.

IMMORTALITY BORES US.
IT'S NOT A MODE FOR GATHERING EXPERIENCE.

                    *

I believe my father's punishment
was exact but too cruel.
Ask yourself, as I do:

Where's your self-criticism, your self-distrust?
Can't you see his boldness?
He went after a god's favorite.

When did you ever ask
so much of yourself?
You'll say he killed himself.

He was a contortionist.
A cannibal digesting a cannibal.
You can't begin to imagine it. Blood shot through

cracks in his skull,
the muscles—he plucked and stripped.
He tugged at his stomach.

I know it was his soul that was hungry.
The soul—which you don't believe in
and yet despise.

The soul kept changing the story.

*

Late in the afternoon,
walking, the daughter comes to

the slaughtered tree.
For years blood has welled in rings

up from the root
where a voice cried out to the daughter

to emulate every form—
even this, even the oak

and its wild spirit:
axes ringing out, the sound

of a child thrown against a door.
Next, leaves thrashing like

a hose against the wall of a bank.
A smoking flood. And then a roar.

Hunger.
Immortal.

Revenge.
Immortal everywhere.

IV.

The Stacks

For the makers of books
the lines into Hell cannot be short.
What little tyrant could each be spinning?
What lavish saint?

How many of these authors doubted
their books would ever be finished?
The woods rustle and thrash and glint
with their murderers on horseback.

The hater of illusion hates even
the smell of decay on these books,
as if decay is an illusion.
These have left us to our ancestors—

in the hollow hull of a tree
where the ribs of a man clatter
like antlers locked in branches.
Open the vise and soot flies.

Deeper in the book a honey petrifies.
On this shelf a deer looks out
through snow-caked eyelashes.
He will not starve

by the work of your hands.
What is my own gratitude worth?
You've found me.
That is our secret.

The promise that's binding.
A route to the hive.
The missing prize.
Someday, my darling, you'll be wise.

You Made Me Read You and I Didn't Want to Do It

At first the page was only a furnished room.
You were the one who furnished it.
A red couch gaudy as a party mask.
Crooked shelving.

And then, after a bit,
weather came into the room.
The clouds "skittering,"
you wrote, "like suds."

And so we pronounced your novel
akin to an ancient travel guide
with its fussy certainty about fares,
adequate hotels, local cisterns.

How can't the book
be shy before our eyes?
It's our fault, not the book's.
It was so embarrassed for us.

The Truth

The counselor disturbs the most children.
The electrician cuts the most wires.
The surgeon cures the most satisfactions.
The florist shreds the most lilies.
The most desperate woman marries the worst candidate.
The worst candidate kisses the most babies.
The banker sits on more debt than the gambler.
The mortician sees more beauty than the beautician.
The lawyer hatches more nightmares than the cannibal.
The photographer closes more eyes than the mortician.
Heaven discriminates more than Hell.
The dog barks at nothing most.
Nothing worries us more than nothing.
Failure worships the most success.
Success knows failure better than anyone.

Procrastination

He couldn't train his mark there
if he found so much as a rip in the paper.
Or if so much as a stray inkling

no more than the width of a hair
ran up a margin.
No, the right page should be boiled,

its source bleached
in branches that thrashed him bare.
Purity gave him nothing to chase.

Poem to the Novel

A fog, a curving road, a woman unfolding fabric.
Later, she pores over specimens from a crime scene.
She thinks memory occupies her life.
And then she is home again, pacing a room
until her husband returns,
and she calls him by another man's name,
and the name is the title of the novel.

Thomas Hardy

There's not a chance.
Too late, he says. But it's never too late
for the poetry of regret.

Pines thicken with this rain.
Always, under complaint,
storm clouds ride above

an ancient forest.
A child close to the earth
listens to the slow revolving of

accidents. Already the child knows
he is a ghost
and must practice becoming himself—

the cliff rising above him will not stop.
He's not one ghost but many,
and there's not enough pity in the world for them.

Dickinson's Day Lilies

She came to me with two day lilies which she put in a
sort of childlike way into my hand, . . . [B]ut she talked
soon & thenceforward continuously— . . .
—Higginson on Dickinson

Humility wasn't enough,
littleness was not low enough;
the lilies she brought might be firebrands,
globes of incense,
torches clapping the air.
She listened to the god of miniatures inside her
and grasped two branding irons,
two distillates of loons,
and she led the lilies ahead of her to where
she was used to finding nothing
much on the other side of a conversation
but an ampoule of air.
She could not let herself tilt
the room in any direction today, and so
she had considered holding two antlers, two thistles,
two mantles of thorns,
she had considered dangling at her neck
a whalebone or
a diagram of the macula like a family
crest to remind herself:
Breathe in,
do not roar.
The lion in the parlor
is playing the lily bearer
with her two jars of bloody milk,
her two bladders of sun soot—
which she can hardly wait to pour
into Higginson's ear.
Only later that night in her bed
must she wonder:
What have I said?
Who saw in me a specimen?
But what had she given away

but a camouflage,
her two broken, golden-necked swans
hissing, fragrance-less.
They weren't notched into her own white paper quite yet.
They weren't what would make her.

Ancient Work

Clytemnestra's Bath

The water splashes up the wall
and threads blood over the ceiling,
more blood than she ever saw in childbirth.
Her hair thrashes with it,
and those summoned
can't know who has been attacked.
Murderers make murderers:
that's all the permission she needs—
the extent of her equality.

Medusa's Mirror

The froth of her mind fleshes into asps.
Who can withstand
the brain's vipers in an uproar,
her efflorescence of nerves?
Think of her pedigree,
the women she's met in history.
Her image is reversed.
If you come to her, you expect to be remembered.

Body Doubles

after reading The Glass Flowers at Harvard—*a photographic album*
of the Ware Collection of Glass Models of Plants

Above the cases howls loud mystery.
—Louise Bogan

The water lily's gold anemone
is sealed with vernix.
Wolfsbane shrugs in a monk's cowl.
Where the gravy boat leaked

this angel-trumpet
shakes out her linen.
On page 109 the chicory frays,
benignly blue.

The meadow lily, pin-speckled
as a military map,
peels back
its landing pads for the bee.

These crafts of our paradise
are fragile,
with nothing about them
of the underworld

where bodies molt and then resume
their shapes,
where pain
is the obscene survivor,

the nerves never entirely break,
the skin between the shoulder blades
clings to the hook, intact,
the brain slides back

into the skull
only to be battered again.
Tyrants of hell,
take your perfection.

We will make our replicas
of the perishable,
delicate and vast,
and they will vanish,

down to the panic grass,
trapped in its fright
wig of snarls,
a model of the inexact,

of the molded, fluted,
painstaking impasse.

V.

The Decorator Crab

The decorator crab
>> lodges on his sticky back
> a patty of leaves
>> and a
>>> gingerly
>>> balanced
>>> pebble stack.

A young father holds the hands
>> of each little girl on
> either side of him,
>> his chest
>>> glitter-
>>> chapped
>>> with nipple rings.

Solomon's Wisdom

Before her child entered her arms,
the mother was split in two.
Lawyers grew out of the floor.
The wise man lifted a sword.
The other woman was in fours.
Wisdom depends on instinct.
Stupidity, I've said it before,
takes ideas.

What Separates Us from the Humans

My tusks,
my marsupial pocket,
        ears that swivel easily,
retractable claws,
        prodigious mating abilities,
an actual shell,
        very fine black feathers.
Everything except for my emotions and their symbols.

"And though she be but little, she is fierce"

—*A Midsummer Night's Dream*

And though her car is old and missing parts,
and though the weeds grow up through her porch,
and though she is acquainted with Revolutionary War re-enactors,
and though she lapses into bouts of cursing,
her cursing is the songline of canaries.

Said Cleopatra to the asp,
said Napoleon to rocky Elba:
Though she is fierce, she is but little.

So the river from an enormous height might seem
the flank of a whippet,
so the bee is more likely to attack us than the whale,
so it's her smallness that makes her so
exactly fierce and confuses all description,
so it's her smallness that gives her
the leaping prowess of a flea.

It's the infant that holds dominion in the nursery.
It's the cutter that intersects the ocean liner.
Like to the ant, the tick, the beetle.
Said the decimal point to the numerals, You all depend on me.
Though she be but little, she is fierce.
Though she be but little, she takes the lion's part.

"And maidens call it love-in-idleness"

—A Midsummer Night's Dream

Others call it love in laziness,
or violence in loveliness,
or affectation on the couchness,
or Won't you ever get up for lunchness,
or I have made an awful mistake, Miss,
or You're prurient, yes you are, Sis,
whereas I prefer beer in beer glassness
and to dwell on the past less.

In old jokes a monarch is referred to as Your Lowness.
Maidens exist, but no one anymore calls them this.
I don't think any less of them. Nevertheless,
this thing you're going to find for us?
It's called love-in-idleness—
which means less is less, unless love is a business
and then we're not talking idleness,
we're talking work.

100 Ways To Say "You're Not Taking This As Well As We Hoped"

What do they call you at home?
You, the one giving a testimonial to dread,
hydraulic engineer of whimpers,
last draft pick of the brain stem.
If you could see the vultures circling your installments . . .
or how the seven deadly sins feel like twelve when you're around,
the seven days of the week: ten Mondays, no less,
or how (upon your arrival)
spring won't get out of bed,
you'd recognize yourself as
a range war on the scalp ridge,
a worry loom,
touch inhibitor, skull sieve,
anxiety gourmet, gravity's soufflé,
absolute ruler of all sinkholes,
fata morgana of the mall,
lotus eater of the dog pen,
sulk kiln, weather forecaster of mood drift,
on night shift with the daylight savings plan,
melancholy's faithful friend.
Your mortgage insurance is too high—
and yet you have no home. Think again!
What's scorched? Your brain pan!
Petit rabies has nothing on you.
You're misunderstood by God himself.
You're lower than Hell's most popular citizens.
You're a chasm's chasm
and nine varieties of meat loaf
in prison, anxiety gourmet, pressure oracle,
flume of spent wishes, what did you expect?
Go a little lighter with the mortuary perfume!
You crept into a gunny sack with an oiled ham.
You're riddled by crossword puzzles designed by ants.
Brain tourist, overfed by inhibitions,
frontloaded by Gertrude Stein in a grain elevator,
tongue gloved,
arm wrestling with a snail—loser!—
auto-da-fé of the forehead,
turtle shuck, nerve ruffles above a neck fringe,
you're the brood mare of brooding's mare.
Weevil of the upper air.

We think it's high time to draft the will,
to get that certificate: Congratulations for smoking
since the age of ten!
Choke hold against the calmest gland,
desperation's telemarketer,
muzzle of the grinning puppet,
laughter's backward twin and grizzle stash.
Where's your mountain ground to ash?
Where's the pinnacle inside your bonnet?
Where's the throne that tipped you off it?
Look! Failure's wearing your boots to the interview!
Dejection's wet ammunition.
Many happy returns to the playground, Grizzly Bear Man.
Display window dunce. Dancer with reluctant clams.
Grand equatorial belt skidding on the floor.
Oyster voted mayor of Grand Forks.
Peacock caught in window fan.
You can't take a little off the top.
Dust handshake.
Spider's back slap.
Your defense team: paper dolls!
Didn't I ask, what do they call you at home?
Napoleon of juvenile detention.
Frankincense of empty arguments.
Mole-spotted mirror of dim hope.
Rind of lost chances.
Silk's nostalgia for the spinning grub.
Spite in a bubbling ski mask.
Disappointment's cheese.
Captain of the drowned lily pad.
You under the bridge with the troll:
your grand prize: toothpicks for one!
Witness to a sea monkey's life span,
grudge spice,
abysmal clarinetist in the marching band,
you might as well be
misery's little handkerchief
and the devil's oven mitt,

a mildewed affidavit against winking,
a ferris wheel in an ambulance,
a ferret in a sleep clinic,
worry's soap scum at the rim of a hat,
wish bone memorial of the Turkey Clan.
It must be dusk with you back in town.
All morning it must be time to go in for dinner.
Knock knock. Who's there?
Nobody. Nobody who?
Nobody who cares about you.
Did I mean that?
What's meaning anyway?
A contagious agent?
Insurance?
Knock knock. Who's there?
Insurance.
Insurance who.
I'm sure it's who you think it is!
It's you!
Why aren't you happy about it?

Higher Society

When God Got Married

She could never be unfaithful without him figuring it out.
The statistics said he would live longer as a result,
as if he cared.

When the Devil Got Married

Hell is the proof.
She raised the roof.
Now it's hotter everywhere.

When Plato Got Married

The bride was a facsimile.
She wasn't his ideal, that's the truth.
What's philosophy worth?

When Aphrodite Got Married

Pity for her husband's career
seared her to the roots of her hair—
until she turned to war.

She never got her arms all the way
around that god.
Now everyone calls everyone a whore.

Soitenly

That I find Larry sexual is not something I would until now be likely
    to confess.
Larry looks as bedeviled as an ambassador or a man with a mortgage.
His eyes want to spring out of his skull,
his hair rises perpetually on end. There's no lull
for Larry. He's well-meaning husband material,
losing every pie fight, dipping low on an aerial,
spitting chicken feathers. Even when he's happy
he looks harried, even when there are dames on his lap.
The gods in heaven confess they make mistakes.
Larry takes it hard. Slapstick.
Everybody says: That's just life, speeded up,
eating the shell of the oyster,
continuing on to the napkin, the plate (it gets worse, sir),
being doused in liquid cement, sat on by a horse.

While Curly is, of course, everybody's favorite,
and Mo is scary,
I mean, truly frightening even,
unlike Larry,
a man you can count on never to relax.
Larry who makes worry a picnic with fire ants,
followed by a hike with bears.
Curly gets all the good lines and swears:
Soitenly, soitenly, soitenly.
What's certain about Larry?
Quiet, desperate uncertainty:
that's Larry's. Which is what I like about Larry.
As well as
the suspicion that frightening him would be exceedingly pleasant.

The Slow Insult

How long did it take crawling the ice floes?
How long on the flesh of the anaconda of the Amazon?
Or else
how fortified the mind must be,
its sentries waving their pikes

until years later
a woman sits up in bed
and recalls a conversation
and how she treated words as
without cunning.

By now the insult is rusted and bent
and dwindled a bit in rain,
and the insult's dart is as curious as
an archeological implement
in a museum.

How good it was late.
How good it was slow.
How it would have lodged in the heart
its poison,
how good for once at last not to be young.

What's the Good of It?

He had short patience for scientific study:
All they want to know is why frogs croak.
It's a philosophical opposition,
his believing in things as only themselves
and the intrusiveness of explanations.
I can't begin to tell you how much he hated ballet.
What's the good of it?
He liked *The Flintstones* and wrestling.
Frogs croak.
Otherwise he liked things that could be
lifted and stacked and put into place.
He thought best with his hands.
He built clocks, cradles, worked a lathe.
He took the world's measure.
He was good and he was of it.

After Four Years

My father wasn't dead after all.
He was only in a nursing home.
Why had no one told me.
I was studying to be a nurse
and with delight quit my studies
to care for him.
Having him with me meant
I was already a nurse.
The sensations of bringing him home—
almost exactly those when my daughter was born.
What tremendous unending energy!
I was sleepless, it seemed, for days.
Why would I need sleep?
The impossible had happened.
Just then I woke.
My daughter was still asleep beside me.
My father was still dead.
But what happiness, unearned,
he must have decided to give me.

VI.

The Changeling

What did I ever do to make them tip
the baby out of the crib and roll me in,
like an acorn squash or a cauliflower

from a garden of imps?
They made excuses for me.
Everyone else wanted a scapegoat.

Goats sing blah, blah, blah.
Blah blah blah, I sang to my father.
Why can't you understand me?

I grew into my own face—
the face of a rat, admittedly.
When it got to be too much,

I tied the folks up
with velcro and ribbon.
I tore through the baby book:

a head, peaked as a dunce
from a bad delivery.
The evidence—a little cap embroidered

with my name. I found her deep in the woods
under a vault of branches.
My first mother rocked her:

a perfect baby, never to grow.
I sniffed the air until that mother
slid me out with a swampy smell,

meaty and sweet,
and dropped me headfirst into a ditch.
She jabbed at my ears with a branch

as if scouring out a pan.
I rocked and swung

until that branch

stuck out from under her jaw.
I threw rocks
until her face was sunk.

And then I turned back and
undid my other mother's hands,
pulled the velcro

from her mouth and throat
—and my father's too.
Hide and seek, you silly girl, they said.

It's only hide and seek.
A children's game
has never been played without

the world of the dead
blinding someone:
count backwards from ten.

The rightful baby that curled
against an elfin breast
withers on the bank of a ditch.

Never again will I prove who I am.

The Mermaid's Vacation

Some of the small things fare well—
grass, for instance,
seems moderately unaffected

although admittedly drowned.
There's that air-chapping new washed lucidity.
Air for air. Air's air.

Blown out from the abyss—
so agitated things won't settle for days,
but keep asking: Who was that kleptomaniac?

What did she take into her big peaked hat?
Why did she boil herself into smoke?
And who belongs to those damp hands?

The tail and not the dog.
And a lovely tail it is,
said the gentleman stranger.

The Outer Islands

No two days went by
when I didn't think of the islands.
When I looked into any distance I found them.
They couldn't be drowned
or carved into coral.
A god was killed on the islands
and a god was born.
That's the least I required of them.

The Bull in the China Shop

For years we carried forks
exquisite as chimes at our necks.
For years we were alert,

our motions light,
without impress. You would think
we should be pocketable,

slim as a chisel by now,
and not horned, not so
thick and heavy-breathing

and big-necked and just asking for it.

Women with Putti

As if they're attachments,
fleshlies.
They're not children so much as sentient
buttocks that float, or
her future embryos,
charging . . .
these soft cloven hooves
turned inside out,
these most buoyant citizens
paddling the canvas
of their lovely grandame.
To look is to
fund a bank of them,
anarchists armed with bows and arrows at the gullet,
honeyed to every pore with mischief,
dimpled with knowledge,
not death's head
but life's head:
the very tips of the nervous system
unfurled unclenched blossomed and given intelligence.

Clairvoyance

Stones, a hill.
What have I forgotten?
Grass silky as cornstarch.
Fog comes under a door. No.
It's not fog, it's smoke.
It's churning, it's water.
The noise is on the other side
of a wall, high in the wall.
Now the sound is off.
And then I realize:
I am inside a dream.
A woman is being beaten.
I can reach my hand out
and the world parts.
The dream is nowhere
but the woman is
in every part of the world.

The Gift of a Birdcage

—for Sylvia Watanabe

It took so long to open the box it came in:
velcro, bubble wrap,
until at last a lantern for air and sunlight came into view,
this cutting lens, this vocal chamber
with not one
breast patch the size of a thimble—

but a sphere of slit air
whittled for traveling,
from which a bird has flown, a bird
once carried in this cage on a pole
and stirred along city paths.
As if a voice only,

a song to be fed.
And now it seems there is no door,
no means of escape—until we make out what's
worked into the design:
the hatch slides upward. Why is it
we can't help but think

of birds everywhere under a dome?
What natural history museum
with drawers of
beaks and hollowed eggs and
abandoned nests was that?
Above us, open wings were suspended on wires.

We had walked into another century's curiosity—
so much rigging and tufting
and rocking above us,
as if Pandora saw first this conflagration,
these latitudes
splintered and bobbing,

before the 19th century cracked into the 20th,
the 20th into the 21st—the counting
never exact, the toll higher than we can imagine,
this dream dreamt in

an elaborate carrying case—
a tiny ghost

beating and pecking
in a swinging bell slicing air,
our wooden sieve
that holds the broth
of a cloud in its small province—
imagine its shadows falling inward.

Assumption of the Jumblies

Their heads are green, and their hands are blue,
And they went to sea in a Sieve.
—Edward Lear

The pig in the cart has long been dead.
The truth is: We jumblies
take on moles and eye patches.

Every waitress approaches us like a nurse.
We sail no more the sea.
Why, then, were we all called in

for questioning? We hadn't known
we were witnesses.
We weren't particularly observant.

Yet it seems we were responsible
for the sieve. The prime minister made his demand:
Give us back our sieve, he said.

There has never been a sieve, we said.
Unless the sieve was us.
We were your sieve, sir.

And at this point we're something else.
We're the distance now.
We're the ones you have to cross.

Undid in the Land of Undone

All the things I wanted to do and didn't
took so long.
It was years of not doing.

You can make an allusion here to Penelope,
if you want.
See her up there in that high room undoing her art?

But enough about what she didn't do—
not doing
was what she did. Plucking out

the thread of intimacy in the frame.
So let's make a toast to the long art
of lingering. We say the cake is done,

but what exactly did the cake do?
The things undid
in the land of undone call to us

in the flames. What I didn't do took
an eternity—
and it wasn't for lack of trying.

Acknowledgements

The author sincerely thanks the editors of the following journals in which some of these poems, sometimes in variant versions, appeared: *The Adirondack Review, American Poetry Review, Antioch Review, The Atlantic Monthly, Barrow Street, Caffeine Destiny, Carolina Quarterly, Confrontation, Denver Quarterly, Double Take, Failbetter, Fence, Field: Contemporary Poetry and Poetics, Georgia Review, Harvard Review, Hotel Amerika, Inertia Magazine, The Literary Review, Luna, The Massachusetts Review, Mid-American Review, The New England Review, The New Republic, Nimrod, Northwest Review, Poetry, Poetry International, Quarterly West,* and *Smartish Pace.*

"Dickinson's Day Lilies" received *The Writer Magazine*/Emily Dickinson Award from the Poetry Society of America.

"'And though she be but little, she is fierce'" received the Lyric Poetry Award from the Poetry Society of America.

"Omnisicent Love" appeared in an artist's book, a collaborative project with Curlee Holton.

photo by Theodora Ziolkowski

Undid in the Land of Undone is Lee Upton's fifth book of poetry.
She is the author of four books of literary criticism, most recently
Defensive Measures. Her poetry and fiction appear widely.
She is a professor of English and the Writer in Residence at
Lafayette College.

New Issues Poetry

Vito Aiuto, *Self-Portrait as Jerry Quarry*

James Armstrong, *Monument in a Summer Hat*

Claire Bateman, *Clumsy, Leap*

Kevin Boyle, *A Home for Wayward Girls*

Jason Bredle, *Standing in Line for the Beast*

Michael Burkard, *Pennsylvania Collection Agency*

Christopher Bursk, *Ovid at Fifteen*

Anthony Butts, *Fifth Season, Little Low Heaven*

Kevin Cantwell, *Something Black in the Green Part of Your Eye*

Gladys Cardiff, *A Bare Unpainted Table*

Kevin Clark, *In the Evening of No Warning*

Cynie Cory, *American Girl*

Peter Covino, *Cut Off the Ears of Winter*

James D'Agostino, *Nude with Anything*

Jim Daniels, *Night with Drive-By Shooting Stars*

Joseph Featherstone, *Brace's Cove*

Lisa Fishman, *The Deep Heart's Core Is a Suitcase*

Noah Eli Gordon, *A Fiddle Pulled from the Throat of a Sparrow*

Robert Grunst, *The Smallest Bird in North America*

Paul Guest, *The Resurrection of the Body and the Ruin of the World*

Robert Haight, *Emergences and Spinner Falls*

Mark Halperin, *Time as Distance*

Myronn Hardy, *Approaching the Center*

Brian Henry, *Graft*

Edward Haworth Hoeppner, *Rain Through High Windows*

Cynthia Hogue, *Flux*

Joan Houlihan, *The Mending Worm*

Christine Hume, *Alaskaphrenia*

Josie Kearns, *New Numbers*

David Keplinger, *The Clearing; The Prayers of Others*

Maurice Kilwein Guevara, *Autobiography of So-and-So: Poems in Prose*

Ruth Ellen Kocher, *When the Moon Knows You're Wandering, One Girl Babylon*

Gerry LaFemina, *The Window Facing Winter*

Steve Langan, *Freezing*

Lance Larsen, *Erasable Walls*

David Dodd Lee, *Abrupt Rural, Downsides of Fish Culture*

M.L. Liebler, *The Moon a Box*

Alexander Long, *Vigil*

Deanne Lundin, *The Ginseng Hunter's Notebook*

Barbara Maloutas, *In a Combination of Practices*

Joy Manesiotis, *They Sing to Her Bones*

Sarah Mangold, *Household Mechanics*
Gail Martin, *The Hourglass Heart*
David Marlatt, *A Hog Slaughtering Woman*
Louise Mathias, *Lark Apprentice*
Gretchen Mattox, *Buddha Box, Goodnight Architecture*
Carrie McGath, *Small Murders*
Paula McLain, *Less of Her; Stumble, Gorgeous*
Lydia Melvin, *South of Here*
Sarah Messer, *Bandit Letters*
Wayne Miller, *Only the Senses Sleep*
Malena Mörling, *Ocean Avenue*
Julie Moulds, *The Woman with a Cubed Head*
Carsten René Nielsen, *The World Cut Out with Crooked Scissors*
Marsha de la O, *Black Hope*
C. Mikal Oness, *Water Becomes Bone*
Bradley Paul, *The Obvious*
Jennifer Perrine, *The Body Is No Machine*
Katie Peterson, *This One Tree*
Elizabeth Powell, *The Republic of Self*
Margaret Rabb, *Granite Dives*
Rebecca Reynolds, *Daughter of the Hangnail, The Bovine Two-Step*
Martha Rhodes, *Perfect Disappearance*
Beth Roberts, *Brief Moral History in Blue*
John Rybicki, *Traveling at High Speeds* (expanded second edition)
Mary Ann Samyn, *Inside the Yellow Dress, Purr*
Ever Saskya, *The Porch is a Journey Different From the House*
Mark Scott, *Tactile Values*
Hugh Seidman, *Somebody Stand Up and Sing*
Heather Sellers, *The Boys I Borrow*
Martha Serpas, *Côte Blanche*
Diane Seuss-Brakeman, *It Blows You Hollow*
Elaine Sexton, *Sleuth*
Marc Sheehan, *Greatest Hits*
Heidi Lynn Staples, *Guess Can Gallop*
Phillip Sterling, *Mutual Shores*
Angela Sorby, *Distance Learning*
Matthew Thorburn, *Subject to Change*
Russell Thorburn, *Approximate Desire*
Rodney Torreson, *A Breathable Light*
Lee Upton, *Undid in the Land of Undone*
Robert VanderMolen, *Breath*
Martin Walls, *Small Human Detail in Care of National Trust*
Patricia Jabbeh Wesley, *Before the Palm Could Bloom: Poems of Africa*